Praise for *CHANGES*:

There is a wonderful sense of poets addressing their place in the world, whether through personal identity, family connections, fitting into society, and so many places in between.

Dagne Forrest, Award-winning Poet

This year's pool of poetry submissions varied greatly, with many unique and powerful voices commanding our attention.

Mason Nunemaker, Award-winning Poet

'This superb anthology gathers some of the best in modern writing from around the world.'

Hugh Riches, Journalist and Broadcaster

OTHER PUBLICATIONS:

Shakespeare In Debt
by Ted Stanley

Who's Afraid Of The Dark – Not Me!
by Sarah Smith

Cows In Trees
by Julian Earl

The Dog With The Head Transplant
by Julian Earl

Leaving
Award Winning Short Stories

Leaving
Award Winning Poetry

Survival
Award Winning Short Stories

Survival
Award Winning Poetry

Stardust
Award Winning Short Stories

Stardust
Award Winning Poetry

Changes
Award Winning Short Stories

CHANGES
AWARD WINNING POETRY
Edited by Ted Stanley

CHANGES
AWARD WINNING POETRY

1st Edition published in the UK in 2023 by
Hammond House Publishing Ltd

ISBN: 978-1-7399985-4-7

The right of the individual writers to be identified as the author of this work has been asserted in accordance with sections 77 and 78 of the Copyright Designs and Patents act 1988.

All rights reserved. No part of this publication may be reproduced, stored in a retrieval system, or transmitted in any form or by any means, electronic, mechanical, photocopying, recording or otherwise, without the permission of the Publisher in writing.

Page Design by Alex Thompson
Proofreading by Jennie Liebenberg
Cover Design by Ted Stanley

Cover Image *CHANGES* adapted by Deborah Geddes. Produced by permission of the artist. All rights reserved.

The opinions expressed in this book are entirely those of the individual authors and are not endorsed or supported by the publishers or their sponsor, University Centre Grimsby.

Contains language that may be considered unsuitable for a younger audience.

Hammond House Publishing Ltd
13 Dudley Street, Grimsby,
Lincolnshire, DN31 2AE
United Kingdom

www.hammondhouse.org.uk

CHANGES
AWARD WINNING POETRY

Enjoy this eclectic collection of poetry that brings together award winning writers from around the world.

CHANGES is the sixth in a series of poetry anthologies, each featuring a different theme and including the winning and shortlisted stories from the annual *Hammond House International Literary Prize*.

Includes the winner of the
2022 International Literary Prize

The opinions expressed in this book are entirely those of the individual authors and are not endorsed or supported by the University Centre Grimsby.

Contents

Introduction • *Ted Stanley*	x
De-grouping • Katy Bienek	1
There might be a letter • Sharon Black	2
My Parents' House • Suri Chan	4
The Keeper • Guinevere Clark	6
Bone Maker • Guinevere Clark	8
Joan, My Stepmother • Peter Clegg	10
Nativity • Alan Coombe	12
Out of Season • Alan Coombe	14
Revolutions • Alan Coombe	16
Water and Fire • Alan Coombe	17
Spell for Single Parents • Kitty Donnelly	18
The Spinning Wheel • Ruth Flanagan	20
Heart of Glass • Jaime Gabriel Gana	24
Glassblower • Anne Hodnette	26
Ordinary Miracle • David Holper	27
Buttermere • Philippa Howell	32
The Discarded Chair • Elaine Howell	34
Displaced • Grazia Marin	36

Contents

Oh • Grazia Marin	38
When • Grazia Marin	40
I Will Change • Howard Marshall	42
Getting to know my father at forty • Beliz McKenzie	43
How's the enemy? • Alison McNulty	44
Dad's Dad and the Duomo • Isabella Mead	46
The Travelers' Hymn • Suzette Orlanes	48
All the clothes you'll ever need • Val Ormrod	50
The Burning • Val Ormrod	52
On a journey • Anthony Powers	53
Between Five and Nine • Sophie Price	55
Neon Slipstream • Paris Rosemont	58
The Death Of A Procrastinator • Guo Ru	61
Along the Spine • Penny Shutt	62
Life and death of a log • Lizzie Smith	64
Meeting My Guitar • Tim Taylor	66
Metamorphosis • Tim Taylor	67
Arms And The City • Tony Trafford	68
pyaar mein phansaaya • Susan Wilson	70

Positions • Roy Woolley	74
In Figures • Roy Woolley	78
Versiyonlarimizi • Cemil Yildiz & Rosalind Fielding	80

Songwriting Category Winners

Tapestry For The Blind • Kirily McKellor	84
Proverb • Jen Emery	86
The Poet Said • Laura Theis	88
Recorded Song Winners	92

Illustrations

Glynne Bulman	x
Marzena Wilkes	4
Jacob Goodwin	6
Rachel Sene	18
Margaret Inkpen	32
Doriano Solinas	50
Howard Halsall	70
Howard Halsall	74
Fabio Sironi	80
Meg Macleod	82

Acknowledgements

Many thanks to the Hammond House team: Alex Thompson, Elis Ballard, Gemma Lidgard, Kirsty Hannah, Deborah Geddes, Jackie Collins, Jennie Liebenberg, Hugh Riches, John Williamson and Glynne Bulman.

Thank you for the support from: Jonathon and Katherine Williams-Stanley, Leanne Doyle, Richard Hall, Rupert Hall, Freya Stanley, Kyle Thompson, Darren Kay, Tyler Kay and Eileen Ballard.

Thank you to the University Centre Grimsby for sponsoring the International Literary Prize and hosting the Annual Literary Festival, Grimsby Creates at North East Lincolnshire Council for sponsoring the Literary Festival, the National Lottery Community Fund for supporting our writers' groups, and the National Lottery Heritage Fund for supporting Hammond House heritage projects.

Thank you to our competition judges: Lynette Creswell, Peter True, Hugh Riches, Richard Hooton, Joe Fuller, Steve Jackson, Sarah Crockford, Matt Wixey and Lauren Smith.

Finally, thank you to all the writers who submitted such a wonderful collection of short stories and scripts. We are sorry we were unable to include more.

CHANGES

Introduction

When, in December 2021, we began to consider the theme for our 2022 Literary Prize, the effects of the Covid crisis and the challenges of climate change were at the forefront of our minds. Little did we know what was coming down the road.

Continual and widespread media coverage can make us immune to the human stories behind major events, trends and tragedies, especially when they don't directly touch our own lives. It is often left to the storytellers, in fact or fiction, poetry or prose, song or stage, in medias res or with the benefit of hindsight, to tell the stories that help us understand and feel the impact on the lives of individual people, families and communities – to show these momentous events on a human scale. Sons and daughters gone to war, loved ones dying alone, coastal communities lost to the hungry tide.

Our 2023 anthologies include the winners and runners up in all four categories together with the shortlisted short stories and poetry. They are joined by winners of the university student competition, the judge's favourite entries that didn't quite make the shortlist and a selection of foreign entries, reflecting the diverse cultures and countries that participate in the competition.

For some it will be their first appearance in the Hammond House anthologies. Others have enjoyed success before, showing consistency in the standard of their work. Some are already successful award-winning writers; others will see their work published for the first time.

The Hammond House organisation is run by fellow writers, industry professionals, university students and local people who give their time freely in a mission to encourage, support and develop literary talent in our communities. The International Literary Prize and annual anthologies encourage writers by providing recognition for their talent and their work.

While we wait to discover what fate has in store for us in the coming year, sit back and enjoy some of the best writing from around the world.

TED STANLEY

"There is nothing permanent except change."
		HERACLITUS OF EPHESUS

SHORTLISTED IN THE POETRY CATEGORY

De-grouping
Katy Bienek
United Kingdom

They're de-grouping
erecting barricades
unseen but felt.

Installing, viral sensors
crossing over coughs
coughing up snakes.

Hissing doubt
amplifying inside –
a collective mind.

Virtuality connects them
the world's shutting down
the world's moving out.

Cases rising like bread
made at home with gloves
bread, they can't taste – or smell.

(ENDS)

Editor's International Choice in the Poetry Category

There might be a letter
Sharon Black
France

in the way the orange trumpets
dip towards an unmown lawn
and lift their filled throats to the sky.
Or in the homemade swing
dangling from the deck beam,
one frayed yellow rope-end longer
than its pair. There might be a letter
in the soft white sun asleep
above the poplar crowns like paper hats
on each side of a festive table.
Another in my neighbour's
seven chickens killed last night, the fox
which entered by the only
unburied foot of fencing in the yard.

Or in those glossy, tanned insurgents,
smiling, perfect teeth, a boy band
raising rifles in the air, posing in their pick-up
as they bump towards Kabul.
Or in the way my daughter hugged me,
slim arms tucked round mine, head
heaped on my shoulder as she left this morning.
There are so many ways to die, ways to love.
The trumpets waver in a breeze.
I am writing a letter
to all my children's children I will not meet.

3rd Place in the Poetry Category

My Parents' House
Suri Chan
Australia

My parents' house is a time capsule
buried deep underground.
The furniture is intact;
my sling bag, a preserved fossil,
exactly where I left it.

At first glance, it looks like
time cannot touch anything here.
Then I notice spots where the light got in:
new lines on my parents' faces,
my grandma's protruding veins.
It's as if time seeped in through the gaps
and cracked them at half the speed –

Which is to say, my parents' house
is also a time machine.
My family sits in the living room,
flipping through memories that aren't mine.
Leaving home is like taking rusty kitchen
scissors and cutting your own face
out of the photo albums.

"There's still time to make more,"
says my aunt, placing a hand on my
shoulder. She calls me by the name
I buried in the garden at eighteen.
There are some things time cannot touch.

My parents' house is a time capsule
and a time machine.
The road that takes you away
carves a new one down your mother's face.
"Oh," she says, as you wheel out your suitcase.
"That wasn't long, was it?"
Her wrinkles all run together
as she scrunches her nose –
a map of all the places she's been without you.

The house calls out from the rear window of your
car.
It sits unchanging, at the end of the road
till distance eventually swallows it;
a time capsule buried into the horizon.
At first glance, it looks like
time cannot touch anything here.
But it can, and it does.

HIGHLY COMMENDED IN THE POETRY CATEGORY

The Keeper
GUINEVERE CLARK
United Kingdom

– breathes under sea,
                lives,
in an alcove by the Atlantic drift.

At Christmas, when the world sleeps,
he wears a human coat, crawls
from a long swim onto landfills to find them –
                little discs, shining
                    under porn mags, stiff tissues,
                        divorce letters, takeaway wrappers.

He is building a gilded palace,
stacking from loss, hears the tears,
sliding desires, clashed loves.

Initialled rings, he'll study, imagine
their names, countries, weather,
shade of their hair on the day's Yes!

Chinked ones he gathered for corners.
Gemmed bands, rare, he'd set
immediately, winking into the door.
In a year, he'd half-mosaiced
the palace floor.

A few he'd smelt for glue.
It was his hardest choice – tossing them
into the steam of alchemy,
kissing the shoot from the star.

And still they come with dawn's
sea shift, from war wrecks, risen
on a crab's claw, dressed on bottle necks,
knotted into a net, floating
into his thin and mythic hands.

Honeyed, fools, white, platinum, dirty,
ridged, muted, Indian, broken golds –
all roll into his golden world.

Each quarter, a single silver ring
washes in. He fishes it out, frozen-bright,
full white, a new dream in his palm, to be

set into the vesica piscis – half-formed
in the queen window. Sea-light,
reaching like fingers though the reeds.

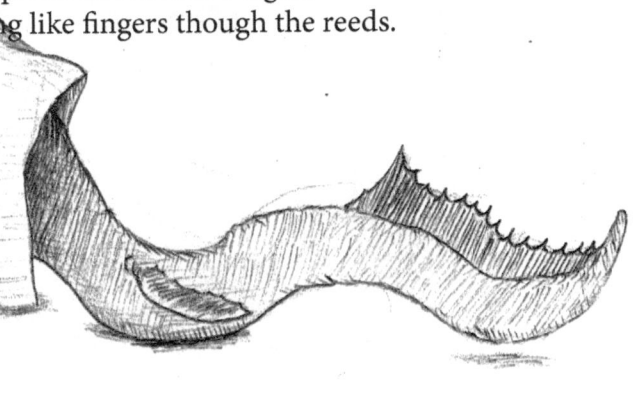

SHORTLISTED IN THE POETRY CATEGORY

Bone Maker
GUINEVERE CLARK
United Kingdom

I remember the grin of that night,
                 our DNA dancing,
    the suck of love
        as we agreed, laughing, to conceive.

Now you sleep in another street,
       our heat strewn
like
   broken   glass
between

        houses.

The neighbour's T.V tearing
through dawn, the postman's gait,
morning tides, milk powders –
I know them all, better than you now.

But I still want to reach

                 through the severing,

snarl
      a rush of expletives
as I feel the rise of our son's skin –
his form still warm like laundry
              in my womb.

This is how I remember you –
in rank fluids, plastic cups,
blankets of vomit,

in the double blood,
young breath
of our twisted love.

SHORTLISTED IN THE POETRY CATEGORY

Joan, My Stepmother
Peter Clegg
United Kingdom

We seldom talked much, Joan and I.
Most times a gentle smile,
a twinkle in the eye sufficed.
Somehow my father used up all the words,
as activist, journalist, author, teacher, poet,
Leaving Joan with silence.
No timid silence this.
Not a holding of tongues
but a bedrock of strength
supporting us when required.
It cannot have been easy
one a teenager

the other not much more
and our mother dead barely a year before.
But silence eased and love grew
and all was well.
So now, as the last words fade and lose their
meaning, what still remains?
silence,
that gentle smile,
that twinkle in the eye
goodnight

Shortlisted in the Poetry Category

Nativity
Alan Coombe
United Kingdom

*With acknowledgement to Christina Rossetti's
"In The Bleak Midwinter"*

The low sun's rays display a river's course.
There is no footfall; the silt is too fine.
Bracken reddens deep and loses its shape.
Frost cracks the Alders' few remaining leaves.
Greylag geese raise a familiar cry.
The ice and the keen wind have seized their wings.

Air's white tallow has frozen this valley.
On its hillsides beaten trails link hay bales.
Shepherds work dogs below a morning star
gathering the black-nosed, green-daubed, Valois
to a sheepcote. A woman shelters there,
questions, hurts, voices fervent orison.

Where do I end for a child to begin,
becoming something more, less, and other?
I am no exhibit, would be no muse
for the poetry of shepherds or kings.
I pray…let me greet my child, take his hand
one moment before this world knows he's born.

This time is as those when eclipses end,
when the heavens host fractured fugues. Skylarks
surprise blackbirds, join exultant chorus.
A new sky's crazed glaze, dipped red, seeps gold from
east to west. East winds seek, the west winds seize,
the last smirr before sleet. The star remains.

Thanks to the Name that we reach this season:
her words carry with wind-eyed swell and snow,
snow upon wood stacked by the cote's high wall,
leeward - haven, a place of praise; blessing
in susurrant word-guessed chant of a child,
and warmth, in the breath of a mother's kiss.

Out of Season
Alan Coombe
United Kingdom

The season's ended. It's easy to stand
on the path. There's no need to step aside,
and allow the hike-clad strangers safe ground.
There is place to wonder where deep sea ends,
and moist sky starts, and not need an answer.

Below, sits the resort, once fishing port,
a waymark-tamed cliff enfolding its cove.
Here, out of season, beached boats, rest on thrift,
hold fast to sand's scrape, shift and shock of shale,
await repair, till pubs serve food again.

Shops, shuffled by, are shuttered, storing stock
till absent traders return in the Spring.
Sharp winds press dunes hard to a workshop wall.
Cobwebbed windows dance the strand's only light,
azure, from salt cast to clay, fire, and luck.

Nearby, a stream brings white spoil from the moor,
Kaolin's waste, flowing like celadon
from inshore wave-break to sea's mazarine.
Clearer lines, of a constant copper tint,
dress the workshop's shelves: the season's last pots.

Coffee mugs have sold well; souvenirs, props
for tourist's tales of their holiday lets,
where flax ran wild through untended gardens.
These flowers float; lend the potter their blue,
for a season, June until September.

Winds drop, stroke the sea to cat's paw ruffles.
Breeze-tipped waves play with the light on their crests.
Inshore, stalks of flax can at last be seen.
Sea-dipped rope is hurled in the kiln. Only
out of season, is such a risk taken.

SHORTLISTED IN THE POETRY CATEGORY

Revolutions
Alan Coombe
United Kingdom

A crystal quiet fell to the waterside. We watched
swallows fly fractured arcs from the stream to wattle-nests,
cursive-looped below the line of a hull's* dry cracked eaves.

A weir slowed the brook's course. We picked stream-gladdened pebbles,
pressed hard to a waterwheel's iron, oak, and elm frame.
This wheel once turned, this hull held, harsher stones, that ground steel.

We'd known white foam crest through the sluice, pulled the tenter taut,
dropped the running stone, geared this wheel to a whetstone's spin,
stemmed the surge from the settled millpond: a final time.

Spinning sandstone - quartz scattered - gifted steel its edge, glazed
the face of blades. Swarf filled our lungs, slowed this, our return.
Bankside, while swallows dipped, we threw pebbles in the pond.

---

* Hulls, here, are not nautical, but are the workshops which once held grindstones to sharpen and brighten blades, on an industrial scale.

SHORTLISTED IN THE POETRY CATEGORY

Water and Fire[1]
Alan Coombe
United Kingdom

Beneath the shale-formed balcony, the pulpit pool
(cut deep by churned pebbles) swirled to check the stream's flow.
We watched, behind the curtain, through the waterfall.

We'd heard a note, below the crest line of this chute.
A second, pitched above the pit's restless murmur,
danced with sunlit water's inner glimpse of fire.

Bulrushes bowed, a wind ruffled the thread-leaved pool,
birthed rapids, pressed the talus, guard of fallen stone.
The pool's bowl stirred to a boil. Reeds swayed, conducting
the stream's surge and swell, its rise to a mud-bank nest.

A Kingfisher took flamed flight.

---

[1] Prompted by Anthony Milner's oratorio, *The Water and the Fire*

1ST PLACE IN THE POETRY CATEGORY

Spell for Single Parents
KITTY DONNELLY
United Kingdom

Take a single magpie feather.
Burn it with a letter
you penned to your younger self.
Mix its ashes with a glass of Irish Sea.
Sip the breeze's brine, metallic
as the signature of pregnancy.
Soar high above the bay
of froths, slicks, ribbons of grey.
Call & sing to others on the wing
those verses of freedom
rehearsed in the gut.
        Though you'll plummet
to your rented room,
sky guano-white, toys bleating
underfoot, those magic hours
will fold you in their plumage.
Ride their thermals,
till your own dawns' break
in the beak of the alarm's plea –
kitt-ee-wake, kittiwake.

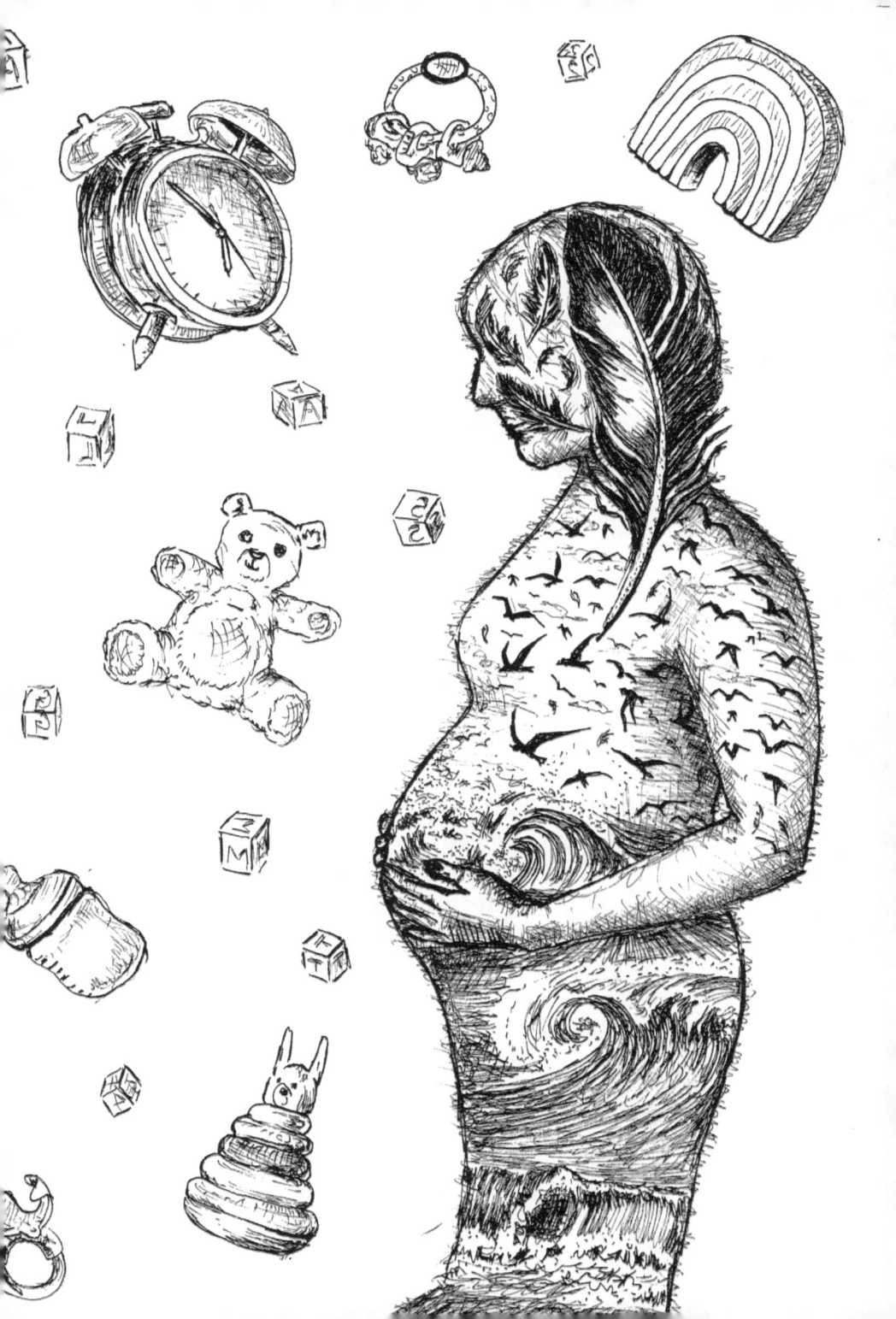

SHORTLISTED IN THE POETRY CATEGORY

The Spinning Wheel
Ruth Flanagan
United Kingdom

Seasons flow like notes and rhyme and
each will come at their due time;
a changing song of highs and lows, for
what one reaps, the next will sow.
Thus it goes that as Earth spins, Winter
is our New Year King,
who rises in a dreary gown of rain-swept
grey and sepia brown.

He brings a stupor in the air; a weariness
too cold to care
and stillness fills the eerie gloom where
thrushes sang and roses bloomed.
Now hungry crows nest in bare trees
while gutters choke in rotting leaves,
As Winter turns the skies to grey and
Autumn's colours fade away.

With Summer's promises long gone,
Winter sings an ageless song
of barren fields and lonely skies and
cheerless folk who hurry by.
Of short dull days and lamp-lit rooms
where light is scarce and night-time
looms.
Of rain that falls from week to week
and housebound months both long and
bleak.

Next he opens Heaven's gate, where
robed like smoke, the cold wind waits.
Then from the chimney pots it sweeps
and howls down the empty streets.
Now blowing all the clouds from sight,
stars twinkle in the freezing night
and in our gardens Jack Frost creeps,
whilst in our beds, we try to sleep.

Then on her sleigh the pale queen rides,
trailing snowflakes in the sky
and wrapped in furs from head to toe,
she paints the world in white below.
Silently, she stops and waits for night to
pass and morn to break,
then glistens in the sun's bright glow as
children play out in the snow.

Now Winter, peering from on high, is
prompted by their joyful cries,
to call time on his bitter keep and rouse
fair Spring from slumber deep.
Soon tiny shoots break through the
snow and in the light begin to grow
and Spring, fresh in a dress of green,
brings with her smile, a changing scene

of nests and eggs and morning dew, of
buds and birds and skies of blue.
Then she opens wide the door to Summer's sun and blooms once more.
So, when fair Spring and Summer sleep
and Winter's days are cold and bleak,
mind not the frost the wind or rain, as
each will spin around again.

SHORTLISTED IN THE POETRY CATEGORY

Heart of Glass
Jaime Gabriel Gana
Canada

There is a patch of sky
that takes its place
comfortably
above my soft glass window

Billowed cloud
Immaculate cotton bloom
It leaves
And another takes its place

A blot delightful onto pale blue
Sea foams
From top
Not bottom

As they pass
My mind is at ease
Pressed against
Warm tinted glass

Yet the sky is out of reach
I hold out expectantly
and yield to emptiness
no air between

Wings I find on my back
from my yearning to fly
Become Icarus
with more troubled mind

I see not feel
as day turns to night
and night turns into day
yet again

Seasons change
I remain the same
Pining for air
beyond crystalline chrome confines

Now it is grey
the tempest storm brews like God's fury
within, without it rages
yet in this comfort I at last yearn to break free

So in this holy hour I steady my strained pinions
as I take one final desperate look
and in shattered glass
I fall and take flight!

Shortlisted in the Poetry Category

Glassblower
Anne Hodnette
United Kingdom

This work is for the optimist.
There's fragility in glass.
Success lies in balance, an even gathering,
smooth rotation, steady breath.

A man could grow old striving,
mixing potions, looking for the miracle
that removes cracks from potash
or searching for some long lost skill

but then there is a type of man,
who, like the glass he blows,
forms and re-forms
in each amorphous moment,

breathes and sweats himself
into everything he does.
Flaws, the catalyst
to try again.

SHORTLISTED IN THE POETRY CATEGORY

Ordinary Miracle
David Holper
United States

You are away in Texas. You went to a dude ranch in some
tiny town with your sister, to make her happy. You do
that. You do that with everyone you meet. You spread
happiness as if it were your full-time gig

to crack open the broken places in people's hearts and let
the sunshine come pouring in.
You have cracked open my heart so many times it is nothing left but fractures--sunlight sneaking

into the hurts. Even when you yourself fractured, and the
surgeon had to scalpel out the tumor,
close up the nine-inch gap in your colon, and the doctors
bathed your body for a year in chemo, even then,

you didn't stop—though you could barely stand. You
gathered the broken women you knew,
threw a party called the Wild Women of the West Wing-
ding, complete with plastic cowgirls,

plastic horses, plastic corral fences. You played cowgirl
music, dancing with those gals
as if it were the best birthday of their lives. I don't even
remember what the party was for,

other than for the chance for you to love them as they
couldn't quite seem to love themselves.
When Mary Jo died from MS, you loved her to the finish
line—and then loved her beyond,

named an hors d'oeuvre in her honor that we still love
eating, all so she will never die.
The thing is, you don't really believe in death, not your
mother's who left you at 13

when the cancer undid her, not your daddy's who two
years back, shattering
your heart into so many pieces of tears—and sunlight.
But I know it didn't stop you from believing

in a place where death has no voting rights. It didn't even
slow you down, not even when
you got a good paying job with two women for which the
word "bitch" was given a special place

in the dictionary. I watched you drag yourself home each
day, beaten and bruised from the way
they tried to make you less a miracle than you are. I tried
to tell you to quit, but you weren't buying

what I had to sell. A month later, even though the other
gal who works there can't wait to escape
the toxic swamp, you turned their two bitter hearts as
easily as if you were commanding the wind

to fill their sails and blow them to a land where they
could learn how to be human beings again.
The thing is, I didn't believe in miracles growing up. I
didn't believe that the lame could walk,

that the blind could see, that oceans could be parted or
that the dead could rise up out of the earth
and shake off their grave clothes and join us for drinks at
6. You taught me how to let go of that belief

in what is practical. You taught me that love is bigger
than all that, bigger than the broken self I look at
in the mirror, the one I had learned to hate because, after
all, isn't that all the inheritance my parents

offered me. You taught me that love is fluent in every
language, knows where it is wanted, which is,
after all, everywhere. I am just trying to say thank you,
even though it took me so long to think of it,

even though I have already said it so often now I am
afraid I have worn down the words like the thinness
of a beloved pair of jeans. Still I am saying it. I am saying
thank you for helping me to become

something so much better than the thing I was when you
washed my feet so long ago in Alaska
—and then rubbed them with oil. It was such a beautiful
thing to do I didn't even understand it then.

Maybe I still don't understand it. Maybe I don't really
understand the miracle that you are, but I going
to give it my best shot. I am going to learn to love you
with the kind of love that forgets itself, shatters

the dam to let the river return to where it belongs, and I
will happily be that salmon that returns to you,
because if anything is a miracle, you are, and I'm leaping
toward you, current be damned.

HIGHLY COMMENDED IN THE POETRY CATEGORY

Buttermere
Philippa Howell
United Kingdom

On long ago fells
In the evening sun
Two ghosts walk home
Chasing their long-jagged shadows
Working their way down
Scree-sliding, stumbling
Grabbing at branches
Laughing among the nervous sheep
Jumping into prints of earlier feet
Splashing in brown-puddled mud

Every time I go back, we are there
It is as if we never left

Through the years we met sometimes
Keeping a finger in our page
Leaving the door ajar always ajar
As wistful wisps slipped in
We toasted our children
But never shared them
And for many years I dared to think
We would walk again
Down to that everlasting lake

But avalanche of wasted time
Rumbles high on those hills above Buttermere
And I cannot remember your face anymore
Just strange things
Like your eyebrows
Your shoulders
And your shoes.

SHORTLISTED IN THE POETRY CATEGORY

The Discarded Chair
Elaine Howell
United Kingdom

Hand turned, carved
sculpted from oak.
I'm no flat pack babes,
I was built by a bloke.

Though I'm no spring chicken
my upholstery is still well-
stuffed.
My Legs long and shapely
all polished and buffed.

So, after seventy- years' service,
how has come to this?
Abandoned. In a car park.
Spurned, cast aside, dismissed.

Where once I was useful
treasured, polished, refined.
I am now a piece of flotsam,
Useless. Worthless. Maligned.

The ousting was sudden and
came as quite a shock.
I am still in fine fettle
not ready for the chop

Perhaps I will be upcycled?
Transformed. Altered. Changed.
Something to grace Sotheby's,
I'm sure that can be arranged.
But, hark, I hear the tumbril
taunting its reverse.
Be steadfast? Be brave?
Bugger that I'll disperse.

Strange sounds, stranger voices
 swarm around, make me shift.
How can it end this way?
Gone. In a twinkling. Tipped.

Displaced
Grazia Marin
Australia

44 days on the water, she said.
44 days with no solid base.
Years in camps, here and there,
To finally get to this foreign place.

44 days of liquid hell,
With waves crashing down.
Tossed about like an empty shell
On sea foam all around.

4 years before, it hit the world,
Pouring lives into a sinking sieve.
No way to rely on any plan.
Italy had nothing left to give.

Flotsam bunched up on rocky shores
To then be factory fodder.
Doing all the dirty chores
At the bottom of the ladder.

40 years later, still not certain.
When did we plant roots to belong?
When did we feel no longer a burden?
Neither one nor the other. It took too long.

No longer Italian but not Australian enough.
Too Australian to be part of the group.
When was the turning point, mother?
When did we rise to become tough?

Nearly 80 years on, we are part of the country.
The xenophobes turn to the east.
New boats with coloured jetsam
'Swamp' the north coast. They are now the new beast.

Shortlisted in the Poetry Category

Oh!
Grazia Marin
Australia

Oh, the righteous are so arrogant
As they praise their 'one true god'.
They sing songs of paradise
Where they know they will belong.
In the competition for eternity
They control your sexuality.
Is the Pill a sin in the Vatican City?
In ivory towers there is no pity
For the powerless and the poor.

Ah, the righteous are such bigots
Doing nothing about their guns.
Their 'rights' are more important.
They must have their fun.
Condemning those who terminate,
Saying babies must be safe.
Will they ever hesitate
To sit above and pontificate
Over other women's tragedy?

And the righteous are so boring
As they are always, always right.
No doubts cut the cold surface,
Writing rafts of rules for life.
They talk of an all-knowing man
Who has some inscrutable plan.
Can we hope to understand?
Well, hear this:
Prayer will set you right.

Oh, the righteous are so dangerous.
When they go far too far.
Imprison women who miscarry,
Or ban blood to save a life.
Do jailing queer and trans
Only keep them from our sight?
Covering women from head to toe,
Then death by stones in the scorching light.
Oh, keep the righteous from me.

Shortlisted in the Poetry Category

When
Grazia Marin
Australia

"Do you believe?
Do you believe in magic?"
Her upturned face interrogates.
I am stopped, stumped,
then sent on a jolting journey across continents
as I gaze at her rosebud mouth.
I contemplate her sweetness and remember the T.V. images.
In my mind I try to answer her guileless query.

I will believe when all children are fed.
When wars are eliminated.
When women are free to walk, talk, sing and dance
And when queer love is commonplace.

I will see magic when children of colour
are no longer scouring medical waste.
When little boys are no longer camel jockeys,
their testicles smashed with each bounce,
for the pleasure of princes.

I will know magic when murders of women and girls
by drug cartels are no longer a thing.
When slave labour and child sex trafficking are unheard of.
When governments by the people are a fact.

But will this ever be, I ask that little face?
No. No magic my little love. But I say to the smiling cheeks:
"Magic is hidden, little love. It may be here, it may be there.
We need to search. We need to make it happen."

She smiles. And there are the perfect white teeth,
her eyes crinkling in the corners.
Will you make it happen, sweet cherub?
Will you use magic and save us all?
Go my little Joan of Arc. Go!
Make the magic for us who have lost our way!

Shortlisted in the Poetry Category

I Will Change
Howard Marshall
United Kingdom

I have not listened to the wind before,
Or the rustling of leaves upon the forest floor.
I have not watched the sun sparkle through the canopy,
Illuminating, as a spotlight, fresh patches of damsel buds
That open their glow of petals hue accessible to the bee.
When trees convers in unison with plants and creatures
Of another world, they pause in silence and quietly listen;
For they stand in harmony and accord, all creatures of the forest.
I have not seen a timid deer, or spied at far an elusive cuckoo,
Or come across a badgers track, or witnessed squirrel in a tree.
I have not seen them, seen not one, but clearly, they have all seen me.
Within the whisper of the wind, passing through the canopy,
Disturbance of the rustling leaves scattered across the crispy floor,
Within that eerie woodland sound when the owl singularly hoots,
Your presence upon the forest floor, to all, has been announced.
I will change and learn the song of wind and movement of the leaves,
And I will learn to stand so still that I may hear the silence.
I will pause in harmony with all the forest's creatures,
And I will stand in unison and learn, that which I have not.

SHORTLISTED IN THE POETRY CATEGORY

Getting to know my father at forty
BELIZ MCKENZIE
United Kingdom

I pick up the Brighton seashell box –
a rare business trip souvenir
delighting your eight-year-old daughter –
and realise how little I know you,
how sparingly we've talked – really talked –
over the years. I piece you together
with jumbled recollections stacked
against blurred markings of four decades.

Now, without our anchor in between
we shift closer. We let mutual grief
enter our conversations. Its waves shorten
the distance between us, help reboot
our blemished pairing. We stick together
like the shells on the box I still treasure:
precious in their imperfection,
slightly misshapen but lasting.

SHORTLISTED IN THE POETRY CATEGORY

How's the enemy?
Alison McNulty
United Kingdom

How's The Enemy?
                              he said.
When Dad asked the question
we all knew what he meant,
his unbeaten opponent,
the ticking mantelpiece clock,
counting down the minutes left –
deadlines to make the best
of the time he'd been given.

Because he asked so often
we ignored him, we were children.
But today, as I strolled near home
wood smoke set off memories
and time's photo album scrolled.
I remember quite clearly Dad
in his chair next to the hearth
in the room corner. Fag ends stacked

in the full ashtray by his side, smoke palls
curled above his raw-boned head –
that burnt-out husk concealed
by his rough-weathered flint hide.
He'd waited too long, ignored
warning changes. The fuse burned
up and precious time was lost.
All that's left is his tar-stained watch.

SHORTLISTED IN THE POETRY CATEGORY

Dad's Dad and the Duomo
Isabella Mead
United Kingdom

He hailed from a land of hapless names:
Hangman's Wood. Mucking. Gravesend. Grays.
And the war led him to hapless places:

Monte Cassino. El-Alamein.
He wryly wrote that he was home from home.
Until he stumbled on Florence Cathedral,

the fairy-tale marble lifting the Duomo
up to the moon. Until this moment
he'd never known the meaning of beautiful.

He'd seen eyes like white marbles, seen rigor mortis
harden bodies to stretchers. No wonder
this cathedral held the marble he tried to remember

for six weeks in hospital with malaria.
In convalescence, he learned Italian, testing the sentenc-
es
and concrete grammar-rules and lyrical phrases

as he lay in clinical white cotton pyjamas
and dreamt of silence. One day the Matron
screamed at a young nurse for a misapprehension:

You've done the bed wrong! What's with you Italians?
and the Duomo was dashed to a ghost of an outline
and white globed eyes floated up, widening before him,

as he, incensed, turned on the Matron:
Apologise now! It's tha' kinda a"itude
that gets us inter weld wars inner first plaice!

The Matron backtracked, the nurse stopped crying.
When he was better the parents cooked him dinner.
Perché sei gentile.[1] *She no longer bullies our daughter.*

It was the memory of the Duomo under moonlight
that made him say it, made him believe
that something could be salvaged from all this damage,

something that could be weightless luggage
to lighten Grays: a tint of moon
in a tale of the Duomo, home from home.

---

[1] Because you are kind.

Editor's International Choice in the Poetry Category

The Travelers' Hymn
Suzette Orlanes
Philippines

The awakened mortal creation emerges
Embracing the finite stupidity of the world
He carries the words from distant lands
Travelling and singing the genesis
This strange world has a strange notes
All he knows is the music of his heart

The forged creation sings words of wonder
He booked here as a singing traveler
The abundance he needs are in varieties
He acknowledges, use and live
This mortal world is sure a short visit
Memories are captured with his thought

Soon he learns the language of love
Pulsating colors of vibrant creations
The color of love is the singing chaos
What is valuable was never lost
For everywhere he found himself
Different sounds brings different ventures

The Creator nurtures everything, he sings
Living, working and visible in every being
That by His hymn the creations move
For He speaks in the language of love
The wind will whisper the sacred tones
The musician listens; follows the north star

The universe will be the musicians' stage
The stars shine and flick to dance
Everything will move in the speed of light
And form the genesis they carried
For the music he carries unlocks hearts
And all creations will groovy dance.

2ND PLACE IN THE POETRY CATEGORY

All the clothes you'll ever need
Val Ormrod
United Kingdom

This is the bright yellow sunflower dress,
carefree and glowing with ribbons and hope,

you were wearing when you first caught his eye.

Here is the wedding dress, heavy with brocade,
and the veil, studded with gleaming jewels,
that you wore a month later, aged thirteen.

This is the silk gown your mother bestowed
for your wedding night, when he raped you twice,
and crowed as he displayed the fresh blood.

Here's the western-style dress with too short skirt
that he made you parade in for his pleasure
in the bedroom, until his desire waned.

This is the shawl used to cover your bruises
the first time he beat you and spat on you
as you lay pleading on the rough wood floor.

Here is the niqab you hid your face behind
when he smashed your nose and fine cheekbones
and split open your lip like a ripe pod.

This is the burka you wore for shrouding
your tiny hunched shoulders and crooked hip
after his boots crunched hard against your ribs.

And here is the white cloth, neatly folded,
ready to wrap your young body, and catch
his tears as they fall into your coffin.

Shortlisted in the Poetry Category

The Burning
Val Ormrod
United Kingdom

That summer my heart tiptoed into dappled glades.
I floated on a magic carpet of love.
When you quick-stepped us towards the heat
we blazed and burned in that inferno,
charred the clouds and scorched the sky.

Autumn cast a chill that dowsed the flames.
Broken wings flapped in helpless supplication.
As we limped away from the wreckage of winter,
cloistering the pain of departure with tissue words,
I packed my heart once more with ice.

Shortlisted in the Poetry Category

On a journey
Anthony Powers
United Kingdom

Today I am on a journey. Yesterday
I would not have dared. Too hard, too long,
too difficult to contemplate. Perhaps tomorrow
I will have need to think again. But today,
today I am on a journey. The wild
garlic scents the wood, reflects the stars.
Today I am on a journey.

Today I am on a train that's travelling
through my mind I thought too hard, too long,
too difficult to contemplate. Perhaps tomorrow
I may have need to think again. But today,
today I am on a train. The bluebell
nods, perfumes the air, reflects the sky.
While today I am on a train.

Now I am entering a tunnel and try
the naming of parts. Too hard, too long,
too difficult to contemplate. Perhaps tomorrow
I will be able to think again. But now,
now I have entered a tunnel. I saw
a tree crowd the air, reach to the sky.
Though now I am in a tunnel.

Naming of parts in my brain may help focus
the hesitation too hard, too long,
too difficult to contemplate. Perhaps tomorrow
I may be able to concentrate on the
naming of parts in my brain. The sedge plant
waves softly, gently through the meadow.
Today is for naming of parts.

Today I realise is not the day I
will solve the problems too hard, too long,
too difficult to contemplate. But I realise
I have made the start I needed. And today,
today I start the journey. The flowers
and the trees and the sedge sense my mood.
For today I start the journey.

SHORTLISTED IN THE POETRY CATEGORY

Between Five and Nine
Sophie Price
United Kingdom

Diabetic teenagers are up to 3x more likely to experience psychological issues than their non-diabetic peers, according to the American Diabetes Association.

I think most people miss life between five and nine
Old enough for memories but not before everything
Goes wrong in year five
New friends because Lottie was a little backstabber
New insulin pen, first school disco
First time my blood sugar went low in school
Certainly not the last-
Day of primary school. I do miss it.
In September.
Message to younger me, you will spend your life explaining the difference between
Type one and type two. That won't change but
Your blood sugar will. Buckle up.
First time going to a theme park
(Remember to take off your insulin pump before going on a ride or else it will break, and you will die)

Once the golden sunset of childhood mellows away
I'm thirteen, on my first ever date.
Blood sugar dangerously high, rather not inject in front of him
(Mostly) all my friends first dates were a success.
New teenage territory explored.

Sleepover. High blood sugar. Insulin. Fuck, too much insulin. Low blood sugar.
Alarm waking my friends from their constant slumber
The disease is constantly changing, the only consistent thing
Is that it will always be there and will always be changing my life.
I should really give up on trying to grow up like a normal person

Everyone's body changes but taking insulin
Makes it harder to lose weight
Fucks sake, even my teenage girl body image issues are plagued
With this.

Age 16, decided to change and stop hating my disease.
Age 16 it goes to shit, why couldn't I just be normal?
Age 12 bored at the routine doctor's appointment
Age 15 having a mental breakdown at the doctor's appointment
Age 17 having a mental breakdown over biology homework.

My blood is 4.9 and dropping right now. Have to prevent death quickly then get back to writing.

Looking back on momentous adolescent changes
There's what happened at Steph's 17th (Which will stay at Steph's 17th)
Reading festival. Going to college.
Oh, and age nine when one day
I was at the doctors receiving the diagnosis
'No, its not because of anything you did'
We were all thinking about what secondary school got put into
I must constantly focus on staying between 5.0 and 9.0.

Shortlisted in the Poetry Category

Neon Slipstream
Paris Rosemont
Australia

You are much smarter than I was
                         at your age. Advanced species
     from Gen Alpha digital
               native plugged in through umbilical
cord wired from birth to absorb streams
           of coded data transmitted through
   a series of 00000000s and 11111111s whizzing
down the slipstream of a dizzying neon
            highway of knowledge, your attention frag-
   mented into multiple split-
                screens bombardment of information vying
                   for space in the impression-
   able spongy terrain of your saturated brain
   s   w   o   l   l   e   n to excess until it can hold no
more – bloated in the bathtub
            as water trickles over the edges –
   careful, or the dam will break
                and you won't be able to control the resulting

                        n
            s   a   i.
    t   u   m
            I stage an intervention; unplug you.
Still, you dream in binary
                    a sequence of alien black and phosphorescent
    green illuminating the infinite
                screen in your mind. Little Alpha
                        your ability to regen. astounds me.
        When life hurls End stones
in your path, you respawn your way through
                            the Biomes in this game of life.
The world is in your pro-controller hands.

This fossil cannot keep up with the speed of your processing power. I smile sheepishly when the first thing you ask is *Have you tried switching it off then back on again?* I think I'm getting too old for this game.
I think I'm ready to power down.

After a quick rebirth, I will regen. new and improved.

Commencing in...

3...2...1...

Press START now.

Press START now.

Press START now.

Press START now.

SHORTLISTED IN THE POETRY CATEGORY

The Death Of A Procrastinator
Guo Ru
Australia

I am a child, so
I have time.
A long life stretches in front of me.
Let the clock tick.
I don't need to do anything right now.

They say I am an adult now, but still,
I have time.
Job opportunities are everywhere,
And I have decades to be a millionaire.
I don't bother right now.

Since when was I a middle-aged man? But still,
I have time.
It's never too late to start a family.
And as for that trip to Europe?
I don't have to go right now.

Wrinkles weave my face now, but still,
I have time.
Who cares about having grandchildren?
I could again be that merry child myself
If the clock agrees to tick back a little bit right now…

SHORTLISTED IN THE POETRY CATEGORY

Along the Spine
Penny Shutt
United Kingdom

I tore myself in two along the spine,
sent one half off to medical school
to make it all add up, this molecular ache
to believe that all problems have their cure.

The gone edge of me
sunk between the ploughed ridges
of cornfields at dusk, flittered in the riffle of open pages
in the May breeze, and sealed itself

between the covers of laminated hardbacks
to be shelved amidst the hush
of a small town library. The gone edge of me fizzed
like that first sip of Red Bull

as the sun rose on the morning
of the exam I couldn't study for,
after an all-nighter in the garden of the house
my dad went slowly mad inside of.

So I made a list in a new A4 lined notebook
of all the things I'd been told
were wrong with me,
categorised how to fix each one,

spent furtive earnings
on a suitcase full of self-help books
that weighed me to my room where I hummed
with the thrill of transformation. I couldn't see

the fragile beauty I see before me now
in the starved cheerleader in my clinic room,
couldn't accept what I was, as that would mean
to accept being unchosen.

So I sent the torn half of me off
to analyse the receptors and traits
that makes it inevitable that you would choose
someone like her, over someone like me

and the gone edge of me untethered itself,
until nothing surprised me anymore
and I asked myself   how long
can I keep doing this?

Shortlisted in the Poetry Category

Life and death of a log
Lizzie Smith
United Kingdom

Three hundred years of life
flickered in the flames
as the log expired.

It squiggled a memorial
in the soot of the chimney,
a burning 'V' of geese above.

Air escaped in a quaver
at the memory of bee buzzes,
honey in its trunk.

In silence it recalled
the anthems of birdsong,
the brush of wings against twigs.

There had even been a buck or two
who'd liked to sharpen their antlers
against its rough bark.

It hadn't been struck by lightening
but had felt the shudder of a neighbour
bowed by a sudden blow.

Then one day it had been chopped off at the roots
which sapped communication networks –
though grooves of record remained.

Once it too had been a sapling
a slim young thing
waving in the wind.

It didn't hurt giving up body –
just felt like a transfer of energy
into the air.

It hadn't been a bad life,
there had been both storms and shine:
now it was leaving, with fireworks.

Shortlisted in the Poetry Category

Meeting My Guitar
Tim Taylor
United Kingdom

I saw the timber: flesh of fallen trees;
the parts, of humdrum plastic, nickel, wire.
I did not watch the hours of work, the art
that breathed into these dead things an essence
of the maker, implanted grace and purpose,
made them something more than an artefact,
neither inanimate nor quite alive.

Seeing the flame that flickers in the wood
reminds me of the smiths who worked with fire
to conjure metal out of stone, creating
from it objects steeped in power and meaning.
I sensed the thread that joins that craft and this:
the gift – hard-won, jealously protected –
of binding matter to a human will.

Possession brings responsibility.
This instrument entrusted to my care,
for all its beauty, is yet unfulfilled.
It has a voice, but it can never sing alone.
Now I too feel the craftsman's burden:
am I worthy? Are these plain hands equipped
to free the music latent in its strings?

SHORTLISTED IN THE POETRY CATEGORY

Metamorphosis
Tim Taylor
United Kingdom

It is the eyes that show it.
Not the arms, tattoed
with lines of boreholes
drilled to sunken veins;
not the body, shrink wrapped
around the bones,
birdlike in its fragility,
nor yet the mouth
with its fictitious smile.
It is the eyes:
look through them
to the hollowness beyond,
the space scooped out
to feed this thing
that lived and grew inside,
injected into him
as a wasp inserts its egg
into the caterpillar
that will slowly turn
into another wasp.

SHORTLISTED IN THE POETRY CATEGORY

Arms And The City
Tony Trafford
United Kingdom

(or the perils of bus de-regulation)

Discreet and unassuming,
The city coat of arms
On every bus
Defined the point
Where you and me and they,
Were us.

Some stripes, a ship,
A fabulous beast or two,
A touch of municipal pride
In the little latin tag,
Those arms embraced us all.

Now, bilious billboard buses
Ply the junk strewn streets,
Old coke cans in the gutter,
Amid the utter clutter,
The sordidness that greets
Us, when who we are
And where we are,
No longer seem to matter
In the individual clatter
Of a million lives.

And those lives grow cold
Now the city doesn't fold
Us in its coat of arms,
And they and me and you
Aren't us.

HIGHLY COMMENDED IN THE POETRY CATEGORY

pyaar mein phansaaya
SUSAN WILSON
United Kingdom

India is a faded memory now
captured in the bedspread
handstitched in Rajasthan
the rug in the hallway
that we never meant to buy
sometimes I wind up the tuk-tuk
let it spin across the floor
relive those hair-raising journeys
I still have the blessing threads
tied around my wrist
securing me to reality
then there are the elephants
all about the house
a remembrance of elephants
I think of the time
we stopped for petrol

when two came lumbering
into the garage
ears painted in pink mandalas
ready for a festival
sometimes I take out the photographs
look at the changes
dip in my toes to test the water
for tears or smiles
come Winter I twist on a pashmina
bathe in its softness
try to catch the scent of patchouli
or make masala chai
to warm my inner self
sip it slowly breathe in its fumes

they lied when they said
time is a great healer
Mother Ganges just gets wider
so wide

maybe I will never touch
the other side again

HIGHLY COMMENDED IN THE POETRY CATEGORY

Positions
Roy Woolley
United Kingdom

for Mavis Ambrose & Betty Woolley

These days I walk to find out where I am
and if some streets don't hold me now

and if I've taken to canals and fields
to find a clearer path between my thoughts,

then it's because of you perhaps
Lance Corporal Hooten, unmet grandfather,

and the chromosomes your absent daughters
ferried through the dark between us.

You went out with your regiment in 1917,
were gassed and wounded twice in France,

and died in '41 in the Kingsway asylum,
your mind unset by details from another war

but calm again towards the very end:
'I've been such a fool our kid.'

I'm decades late I know but here at last
to trace those roots inside my breath,

conscious of just where I stand
not least because the ground is so uneven

unlike the 'Sixties streets enclosing it.
What was here in your day? Before the concrete set

and made the sinuous hills one fixed thing?
I'm drunk on what I'll never get to know

but can't step back from dreaming
how it animates the here-and-now

to yield a sense both clear and double-edged
we're falling faster than before again.

There are sounds of traffic in the pure wind.
The lights in the city are echoed in brass.

There is a laurel tree and a rook watching
how everything moves backwards through time

to a sea-bright space where two men stand
before one falls and one turns back.

Shortlisted in the Poetry Category

In Figures
Roy Woolley
United Kingdom

for Sarah Lawson Welsh

They filmed the scenes her paintings had inspired
before the demolition work began in earnest
and even frames they'd later edit out
to smooth the changing shapes their stillness made
might lead me back again to what she was
and all those hours she'd slowed through drifts of paint
to fix their molten colours outside time.
She'd stop sometimes, light up and turn away
to let what wasn't finished have its say
between the canvas and her yellowed hand
alive to every echo seeping through.
'You work to let the clearest things find you.'
 - Limehouse, a week before the Poll tax riots.
I'd walked from Holloway along canals
I couldn't know would feel like home so soon
and found the metal doors near the towpath
and breathed what waited for me there
to conjure it again with spells of water
each time I'd visit. The city aged,
the bombsites cleared away like ruined paper
to hold the motile silver walkways
she'd sketch before five hours' work on canvas.

Her lunch was coffee heated on a Primus.
I remember evenings filled with Boulez,
the Barraqué concerto, the trippy winter sunsets
before they blocked and drained the canals
and how her girlfriend (nude, descending)
once stopped the room with Wyatt's Shipbuilding.
I'm tracing sparks that set all this in motion
falling backwards through an empty page
towards her final abstracts done with stolen ink -
those tapering antennae, a black star's
cylindrical shadows, a seething crowd
heading nowhere but the paper's edge -
'Image not word.' Her acrobatic smoke
was seamed with light. 'It's not a Rorschach test.'

HIGHLY COMMENDED IN THE POETRY CATEGORY

Versiyonlarimizi
CEMIL YILDIZ & ROSALIND FIELDING
Turkey/France/UK

How do we stop, measure, define
Nasil durdururuz, yada olcebiliriz, tanimlayabiliriz
Our infinite variations,
Bizim sonsuz versiyonlarimizi,
And how do we understand
Ve nasil anlariz
What else changes when we do?
Neler degisir biz degistigimiz zaman?
Does the smell of our skin change
Tenlerimizin kokusu değişir mi
In a different season in a different country,
Farkli bir ulkenin farkli bir mevsiminde,
And what did summer smell like where you were born?
Ve yaz nasil kokuyordu biz doğduğumuz zaman?
If you move across mountains, seas, city streets
Eger daglari, denizleri sehrin sokaklarini asarsan
By choice,
Kendi secimin ile,
Does it change you the same way as a
Degistirir mi seni oldugundan farkli bir hale

Journey you didn't want to make?
İstemedigin seyahet?
Do the different languages you meet,
Karsilastigin farkli diller
Percolate through you?
Süzülerek gecer mi bedenin den?
Or are they just the signs of a culture
Yada onlar sadece bir kulturun isaretleri mi
You're trying to greet?
Senin selamlamaya calistigin?
I write every word of change, variety, difference,
Degisimin her kelimesini yazarim, cesitlilik, farklilik,
As I move with the minutes and days
Dakikalarla ve gunlerle hareket eder gibi
That mark how far I've come from where
Iste bu işaretidir ne kadar uzaga geldigimin

I started.
Basladigim yerden.

SONGWRITING
LYRICS CATEGORY

1st Place in the Songwriting Category

Tapestry For The Blind
Kirily McKellor
Australia

She weaves the scene with peaceful purpose
With indigo and navy blue
They ask her for whom she weaves
She replies, "not you"

She weaves the scene with burning passion
With crimson and maroon
And this part of the tapestry
Is just her own

For days and weeks and months
She sits by the window
Weaving until dusk
At night she dreams of scenes to add
To her tapestry for the blind

She weaves the scene with endless yearning
With emerald and forest green
They understand not why she weaves
What will not be seen

She weaves the scene with final tones
With mahogany and umber
So the close of her cryptic work
Leads her into slumber

For days and weeks and months
She sat by the window
Weaving until dusk
At night she'd dream of scenes to add
To her tapestry for the blind

The blind, they came en masse to see her tapestry
The seeing came as well, to see how this could be
The blind began to touch, and they began to feel
The seeing stood and watched, as the blind began to kneel

They felt her peaceful purpose in the absence of all fear
They felt her burning passion in the tautness of each tier
They felt her endless yearning with the grace of every glide
They felt her final tones in the precision of each side

For days and weeks and months
The blind sat by the tapestry
Feeling until dusk
At night they would dream of
Another tapestry for the blind

2ND PLACE IN THE SONGWRITING CATEGORY

Proverb
Jen Emery
United Kingdom

Better safe than sorry? My god –
would you rather never stray
from your fireside, or ever light a fire
for fear of sparks? Would you really rather stay
where every wall is magnolia,
every show a mediocre repeat,
every conversation well-worn?
Is that safety? Or is that defeat?

Better safe than sorry means
that all of your friends look like you
and all your opinions are borrowed
and you never try anything new.
You miss out on the salt joy of oysters,
the thrill of being lost in a crowd
the hit of an ice cold martini
the chest-thump when the music is loud.

Better safe than sorry means
never getting lost,
it means money stuffed under the mattress
and forever counting the cost
instead of living the moment
and pressing your foot to the floor
and learning to dance and taking a chance
and rolling the dice just once more.

Better safe than sorry squeezes
your heart in its scared little fist
and whispers that it will protect you
from moments just like this.
Is it safety or is it cowardice
to just sit there, waiting to rot?
You're not sure you can pluck up the courage, but surely
courage is all that we've got?

You call me foolhardy, but darling,
I'm hardly anyone's fool,
and I'd rather be sorry than safe if safe means
always playing it cool.
I'd rather mark every adventure
with one more line on my face.
I'd rather stay up after midnight,
I'd rather be sorry than safe.

I'd rather make dreadful decisions
than wait for them to make me.
I'd rather be sorry than safe.
I'd rather be broken and free.

3RD PLACE IN THE SONGWRITING CATEGORY

The Poet Said
Laura Theis
United Kingdom

I have made a decision
I think all should be forgiven
I have to move on
Far beyond

See this was never a prison
Just some bodies we lived in
No need to find out
What went wrong

So thank you very much
For being so easy to give up
The poet said the things that scare us
Are things that really want our love

They're the running out of days
And they're death and decay
And they're friends that drift away
But in the end it's all a game

So I've made an incision
I think all should be forgiven
I am gone now
Far beyond

Look this was never a prison
Just some bodies we lived in
No need to waste
Another song

So thank you very much
For being so easy to give up
The poet said the things that scare us
Are things that really want our love

They're the running out of days
And they're death and decay
And they're friends that drift away
But in the end it's all ok

I used to do things for a reason
I'd rather do them just because
I hope today's the last time
I felt this unrequited love

Thank you very much
For being so easy to give up
The poet said the things that scare us
Are things that really want our love

Like the running out of days
Death and decay
And the friends that drift away

SONGWRITING
RECORDED CATEGORY

1st Place:
Wake Up To Reality
Penelope McMorris
France

2nd Place:
Change
Sharam Gill
United Kingdom

3rd Place:
Lonesome, Lovesick And Cold
Robert Neil and Scott Nicol
Scotland

Listen to the songs at:
www.hammondhouse.org.uk/music

Hammond House Publishing is a social enterprise membership organisation founded by students at the *University Centre Grimsby* and run by volunteers. We aim to encourage and support creative talent in art and literature, providing opportunities for members to develop their skills, publish their work and follow a successful literary career.

Members benefit from reduced competition entry fees, author profile page, and the chance to participate in our range of cultural activities.

Our annual writing competitions and anthologies bring together some of the best writing talent from around the world. So far we have published over 200 writers from 28 countries.

Our literary activities support the work of other Hammond House organisations to address loneliness and isolation and promote positive mental health in both urban and rural communities.

www.hammondhousepublishing.com

Hammond House is a not-for-profit group of community organisations dedicated to supporting and encouraging creative people across all disciplines of arts and culture.

Our community outreach programmes contribute to easing loneliness and isolation, and promoting positive mental health.

Hammond House Publishing
House anthologies and an annual International Literary Prize

Hammond House Productions
TV programmes, documentaries and music videos

Hammond House Writers
Support and wellbeing for writers and writing groups

Hammond House Music
Featuring original music from talented singer songwriters

Hammond House Gallery
Featuring original work from Lincolnshire artists

Billboard TV
Arts and Culture channel covering Lincolnshire and East Yorkshire

Clee TV
Community TV channel for North East Lincolnshire

The Heritage Channel
Celebrating our local history and heritage

Book the Band
Platform showcasing local bands, solo artists and music venues

www.hammondhouse.org.uk

2022 International Literary Prize

The seventh year of our international literary prize saw a record number of entries spread across five continents.

1st Place	Spell for Single Parents	Kitty Donnelly
2nd Place	All the clothes you'll ever need	Val Ormrod
3rd Place	My Parents' House	Suri Chan

This years' judges were:

Dagne Forrest
Mason Nunemaker
Jean Cooper Moran
Steve Jackson

Changes theme song, written by Ted Stanley and performed by Rachel Makena.

www.hammondhouse.org.uk/competitions

2022 International Literary Prize
Songwriting Category (Lyrics)

The seventh year of our international literary prize saw a record number of entries spread across five continents.

1st Place	Tapestry For The Blind	Kirily McKellor
2nd Place	Proverb	Jen Emery
3rd Place	The Poet Said	Laura Theis

This years' judges were:

Lynne O'Neill
Caroline Johnstone
Malcolm MacFarlane
Tyrolin Puxty
Steve Jackson

Changes theme song, written by Ted Stanley and performed by Rachel Makena.

www.hammondhouse.org.uk/competitions

2022 International Literary Prize
Songwriting Category (Recorded Song)

The seventh year of our international literary prize saw a record number of entries spread across five continents.

1st Place	Wake Up To Reality	Penelope McMorris
2nd Place	Change	Sharam Gill
3rd Place	Lonesome, Lovesick And Cold	Robert Neil and Scott Nicol

This years' judges were:

Lynne O'Neill
Caroline Johnstone
Malcolm MacFarlane
Tyrolin Puxty
Steve Jackson

Changes theme song, written by Ted Stanley and performed by Rachel Makena.

www.hammondhouse.org.uk/competitions

2023 International Literary Prize
Poetry Category

1st Prize	£500
2nd Prize	£50
3rd Prize	£20

Worldwide publication for the shortlisted poems

Theme: FATE
One poem up to 40 lines
Entries open from 22nd February 2023
Submission deadline: 30th September 2023

Theme Song: Between the Lines
www.hammondhouse.org.uk/music

OTHER 2023 COMPETITIONS:
International Short Story Prize
International Scriptwriting Prize
International Songwriting Prize

www.hammondhouse.org.uk/competitions

 University Centre Grimsby

The University Centre Grimsby, as part of the Grimsby Institute, is built on high expectations, a focus on learning, commitment to achievement and an engaged, practical education for all students.

A wide range of degree level courses are available including BA (hons) Creative and Professional Writing.

www.grimsby.ac.uk

www.ingramcontent.com/pod-product-compliance
Lightning Source LLC
Chambersburg PA
CBHW020542080526
44583CB00013B/947